TENNIS
Weaknesses
& Remedies

By PAUL METZLER

STERLING
PUBLISHING CO., INC. NEW YORK

Oak Tree Press Co., Ltd.
London & Sydney

BY THE SAME AUTHOR

Advanced Tennis
Getting Started in Tennis

Athletic Institute Series

Baseball	Gymnastics
Basketball	Table Tennis
Girls' Basketball	Tumbling and Trampolining
Girls' Gymnastics	Wrestling

Copyright © 1973 by Paul METZLER
Published by Sterling Publishing Co., Inc.
419 Park Avenue South, New York, N.Y. 10016
British edition published by Oak Tree Press Co., Ltd., Nassau, Bahamas
Distributed in Australia and New Zealand by Oak Tree Press Co., Ltd.,
P.O. Box 34, Brickfield Hill, Sydney 2000, N.S.W.
Distributed in the United Kingdom and elsewhere in the British Commonwealth
by Ward Lock Ltd., 116 Baker Street, London W 1
Manufactured in the United States of America
All rights reserved
Library of Congress Catalog Card No.: 73–83459
ISBN 0–8069-4060–3   UK 7061–2472–3
4061–1

CONTENTS

INTRODUCTION

You've played a fair amount of tennis, perhaps even a lot, but something is holding you back—a weakness or two in your game. These weaknesses are robbing you of a satisfying all-round feeling of confidence. You've played enough to know what you want—to be a consistently strong player, always able to give a good account of yourself. If you could do this you wouldn't worry before matches or before a social game with a number of onlookers.

You've decided to be your own analyst and sort it out yourself. That is what this book aims to help you do. Once you're sure you're right, you can forge ahead. Here, each stroke is taken as being someone's weakness, and you can apply the information that helps to develop your own game.

Knowing the game thoroughly will not encumber you with thought while in the midst of trying to play a fast ball, and throw your timing off. It is more like recognizing a card in a mis-deal. If you catch a glimpse of the ace of spades you know it. You don't have to think about it.

PAUL METZLER

1. THE FOREHAND GRIP

ONCE UPON A TIME tennis writers used to declare that any grip was correct if it felt comfortable, but this opinion no longer satisfies everyone. For many years now, proponents of the Continental and the Eastern have been debating their relative merits. Possibly more has been written about the forehand grip than about any other aspect of tennis. This fascinates some people, but confuses others.

This chapter will probably provide enough detail and explanation of the grip to satisfy both groups. Its main purpose, however, is to help those players who feel their forehand grip may be a weakness and wonder every now and again if they should alter it.

Basic Grip, Variations and Names

Now that freak styles and methods of play have almost disappeared and tennis has become more or less standard, the basic forehand stroke amounts to a horizontal or sideways swing made at about waist height. Therefore, any forehand grip that allows you a comfortable waist-high drive is all right.

Nevertheless, forehand grips vary widely. The wrist can be as far behind the handle as possible (Western), or its position may progress counter-clockwise round the handle until it is completely on top of it (Continental). The basic reason for different players naturally using different grips is that they find it natural to meet the ball in different positions in relation to their bodies.

Please get your racket out and follow this through. Stand sideways to an imaginary net, meaning, if you are right-handed that your left hip is closer to the net. If you like hitting the ball a foot or more in front (nearer the net) of your left hip, you are using a Western grip. If a little less far in front, your grip would be Extreme Eastern. If a few inches beyond your hip, or about opposite it, Eastern. From a little behind it, Australian, and a little farther behind yet, Continental.

The exact position in which you meet the ball with any particular grip will vary a little, depending on how much you naturally bend your wrist.

Now that you have this basic concept of the relation of one grip to another by ball position and by name, please look at Illus. 1–5. Your first glance through them will show you that they fit the basic explanation given above.

Now please read and follow through on your racket handle all the text associated with these five figures. Take your time because there's a lot of information there. It makes the rest of the chapter easy to follow.

TO VIEW THESE DRAWINGS:

Your racket is parallel to the ground and you are looking down at the handle's top surface and its two upper bevelled surfaces. The short strings are pointing straight down and the racket face is square to the net.

Illus. 1-5 show the counter-clockwise progressions of:
  Palm — from under the handle to on top of it.
  Wrist — from behind the handle to on top of it.
  Thumb and Forefinger ''V'' — from almost the rear surface to the left bevel.
  Base Knuckle of Index Finger — from lower right bevel to upper right bevel.

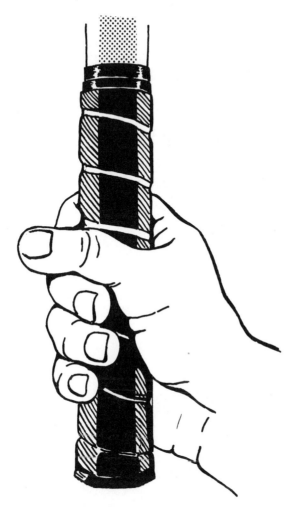

Illus. 1. WESTERN FOREHAND GRIP: Your palm is mainly under the handle and your wrist behind it. The ''V'' formed by your thumb and forefinger lies on the handle's upper right bevel or even on its rear surface.

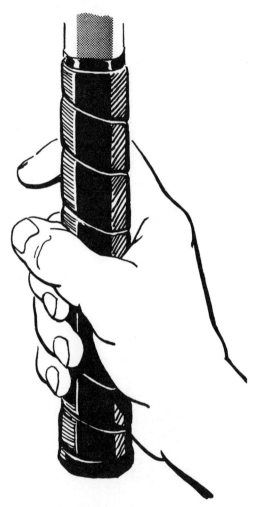

Illus. 2. EXTREME EASTERN FOREHAND GRIP: The ''V'' lies somewhere on the handle's upper right bevel. Basic features of all Eastern grips, including this Extreme version, are that your palm and wrist feel solidly behind the handle and that your large index knuckle presses against the handle's rear surface.

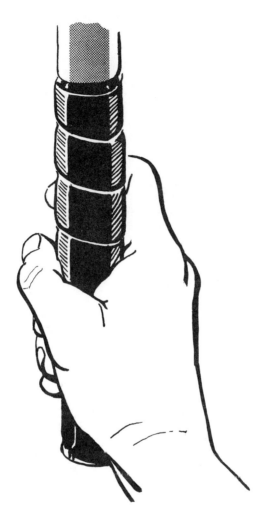

Illus. 3. EASTERN FOREHAND GRIP: Your palm and wrist feel solidly behind the handle and your large index knuckle presses against the rear surface. This drawing shows the thumb and forefinger "V" lying in the middle of the top surface of the handle, but it is still an Eastern grip if this "V" lies anywhere to the right of center on the top surface.

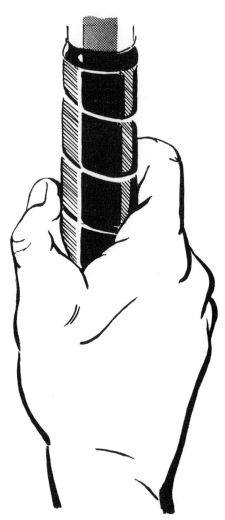

Illus. 4. AUSTRALIAN FOREHAND GRIP: The Eastern grip (Illus. 3) has the thumb and forefinger "V" lying in the middle of the handle's top surface. Moving this "V" to the left counter-clockwise brings your palm and wrist towards the top surface of the handle so that they no longer feel solidly behind it. Such a grip is not yet Continental (Illus. 5), but it is certainly not Eastern.

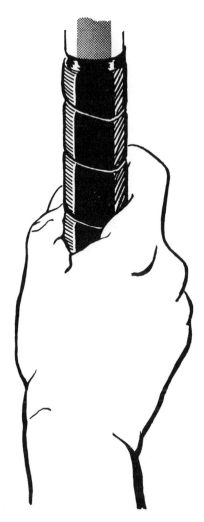

Illus. 5. CONTINENTAL FOREHAND GRIP: Proceeding from Illus. 4, the ''V'' is now on the left bevel, bringing your palm and wrist definitely above the handle, in contrast to their Eastern position of behind the handle. The Continental grip gives you less forward power than the Eastern but, if well used with a free wrist, it allows great dexterity in play.

Western and Continental

Having studied Illus. 1–5, you will probably agree that the Western, Illus. 1, is extreme. You can bat down short high balls with it, but you can't reach far, and you feel clumsy with it against low balls. The Continental, Illus. 5, would be extreme if you kept your wrist stiff throughout the stroke. Try it. You see that the racket face slopes back and also that you hook the ball rather than stroke it. With knees well bent it may be all right for lifting up a low ball, but a grip like this would be almost useless against high balls or fast rising-balls.

Extreme opponents of the Continental grip choose only to describe it in this extreme stiff-wristed form. Its supporters then describe it in its free-wristed form, when it becomes the most flexible of all forehand grips for low balls, wide balls, and those that get behind the player. Its critics then say that it places too much strain on the wrist and that it has little power against high balls. Defenders counter by saying that playing tennis develops a strong wrist, and that a good player can take the ball on the rise, thereby preventing it from being high. Opponents reply that the Continental is a grip for champions only, and then only some. Supporters conclude by inviting critics to look at some of these champions, such as Rod Laver!

To sum up:

■ The Western grip is too extreme.

■ The Continental should be called the Controversial Continental.

■ If you use the Continental and are comfortable with it you are not, repeat *not*, using an incorrect grip.

■ If your Continental forehand is literally weak, this grip is too much for you to handle and it is therefore a weakness in your game.

Extreme Eastern

The Extreme Eastern grip (Illus. 2) signifies power. You have to run farther to get behind the ball, to drive it, than is necessary with a Continental grip, but it produces a forehand that is never physically weak.

Just the same, this grip is a crossbreed—as indicated by its having an adjective to qualify its name. It tends to produce a player with a strong forehand and a weak backhand. The reason is not hard to find: the EE forehand grip calls for a greater change of grip than any other if you are to have an adequate backhand grip.

The Continental requires little change for a backhand, and some players make no change at all. The Australian is close and the Eastern not far away. The Western has its own backhand grip: turn the racket head over the top, and, adjusting a little for comfort, use the same face of the racket for both forehand and backhand. The EE has the greatest change and, as a result, most of its users change grip only part of the way. They use a grip that is only the backhand equivalent of the Australian forehand grip, Illus. 4, or even the Eastern, Illus. 3.

However, if you are an EE player, again you are not using an incorrect forehand grip.

Eastern and Australian

These are the two middle grips. They are used by the greatest number of players, by far, particularly the Eastern. Neither has any intrinsic weakness. However, they are by no means the same thing. With the Eastern you have a feeling of being *behind* the ball, and with the Australian, more *beside* it.

Altering Your Forehand Grip

Altering your forehand grip is the trickiest thing you can contemplate doing, because your forehand is your most natural and individual shot. If you have, say, a strong Extreme Eastern forehand and the associated inadequate backhand, it is almost certain you would be wiser to speed up your change-of-grip than to alter your forehand grip. Strengthening a weakness should not involve weakening a strength.

Nevertheless, for one good reason or another you may wish to experiment at least with an alteration. Here is some idea of what you can expect to find.

When you swing your racket about without a ball, all grips feel comfortable, and so will the one you are proposing to experiment with, too. However, when you play against a ball, a new grip will have little chance of feeling comfortable unless you allow for the different position in which you meet the ball in relation to your body.

Extreme Eastern and Eastern are associated: you are behind the ball. Australian and Continental are associated: your palm is towards the top of the racket handle. If you alter from EE or Eastern towards Australian or Continental you will feel weaker, certainly at the start, perhaps always. An Eastern supporter would say that without question, you will always feel weaker, but that would not be impartial. However, there is no reason for any Eastern player to change to Continental.

If you alter from Continental to Eastern you will feel stronger, but, perhaps, by comparison, somewhat clumsy at first. This alteration is the one most commonly recommended by coaches, but coaches do not interfere with a pupil who has a strong and natural Continental forehand. If the forehand is weak the grip is normally Continental, and then coaches will recommend an alteration to the less demanding Eastern. Some, less drastic, may recommend that the alteration be only from Continental to Australian.

If you are a Western player your game will be strong, but you may feel your grip restricts you for all-round play. If you have both a Western forehand and backhand (meaning that you use the same face of the racket for both) any alteration will be drastic. In almost every case it would be stronger and more natural to stay as you are. The Western style may be too restrictive for the speed and variety of championship play, but it offers strong club play.

If you have a Western forehand but you have to make a very large change of grip to play a backhand with the opposite face of your racket, the alteration you probably have in mind is to an Extreme Eastern forehand. Very little trouble here. This was the alteration made by the great Donald Budge. He improved his forehand greatly. While he still had to make a fairly large change of grip to have an adequate backhand grip, he made it and produced the most powerful backhand in the game's history.

You now have all the information and can experiment and come to a decision. If your grip is Continental and your stroke weak you will probably alter it. If your forehand only is Western you will probably alter it to Extreme Eastern. Other than that it is more likely you will realize your forehand grip is better than you thought it was. So your grip won't alter, but your confidence will.

2. FOREHAND FIRMNESS

MANY LEFT-HANDERS revel in their strong forehands, and a few right-handers also bring this shot into play again and again, because it is an outstanding part of their game. In fact, most players have a forehand that is a strong shot—even though it may not be outstanding in their general all-court play. This chapter is concerned with those less fortunate, who dread playing a forehand. If it is weak or erratic, opponents will sense this and choose to rally even slow shots to it. This makes the owner of a poor forehand feel mentally self-conscious, and his stroke becomes either cramped and unnatural or wild and desperate. No wonder his pre-game outlook is mainly one of apprehension. It is a terrible state of affairs.

Lost Confidence

Much has been said and written about the forehand in general that will undermine the confidence of anyone who so much as feels his forehand may be somewhat suspect. And if he feels this way, it *is* suspect. Let's have some of these remarks out in the open and face them.

■ The forehand is the easiest shot to learn, but also the easiest to go astray and the hardest to regain.

■ It is more difficult to coordinate the forehand because it is the least compact of your strokes in relation to your body.

■ You tend not to turn sideways to the net as you should, and as you do with a backhand, because your forehand footwork is less positive than your backhand footwork.

■ Because of your less positive footwork, your forehand tends to turn your body round before you have hit the ball properly.

■ You don't watch the ball as well as on the backhand, because you don't drop your head down naturally as you turn to play the stroke.

■ A forehand grip is not as strong in itself as a backhand grip, so you need more swing for the forehand, and this makes your timing and your control more difficult.

■ Your grip is too Continental, so the racket face is open and you hit the ball up and out. Or, your grip is too Western, so you hit down and too short. Use an Eastern grip and all will be well.

■ So you use an Eastern. You then realize that all your other shots are made with more or less the same grip: Continental for serve and volleys and Continental with thumb advanced for backhand. There is only one stroke with a grip all its own—your forehand.

■ Your wrist tends to be floppier on the forehand, so you may flick at the ball instead of stroking it.

It is a depressing list.

Remedy

Perhaps, if you have not previously been aware of one or two of these things, eradicating them will be enough to correct your forehand and give you confidence in it. On the other hand, if this list convinces you that the forehand is tennis's most complicated stroke, you begin to wonder how even a beginner can play it.

There is your clue. When a beginner is playing his forehand, at least he is uncomplicated and natural. You can't be, if you try to keep the whole list of worrying points in mind while you are playing a moving ball with the very stroke you lack confidence in.

Forget about your stroke for a while, and instead concentrate solely on ball and strings.

The Ball

First, the ball. You know very well that you must watch it, and just to say this is unconvincing and perhaps boring. Since watching the ball is so important, and so easily forgotten, you need to have your own chosen method of doing it. Here are some:

■ Watch the ball consciously. When you know you're watching it you see it more clearly.

■ Watch the ball the whole way from the other end of the court. When you do this it appears to be much slower and you feel smoother and more comfortable.

■ Watch the ball especially after its bounce. This gives you something to concentrate on. It also tends to make you lower your head a little and prevents the common forehand fault of lifting your head too soon. Moreover, it helps you to settle into a comfortable rhythm.

■ Stop the ball with your eye. Just below the top of its bounce the ball travels at its slowest speed relative to the path of your racket in its sideways or horizontal swing. Your concentrated gaze can almost make the ball look as though it had stopped—and then you can sweep it away.

■ Watch the ball right on to your strings and then hit it.

All these methods are sound, though the last two fit in with dropping-ball rather than rising-ball play. Try them and choose one. Take it onto the court with you.

There is yet another method of watching the ball. This entails watching the point of contact until after the ball has gone, and those who do this claim that it gives them great concentration for backcourt rallying.

One last aspect of ball watching is strictly post graduate. Champions don't always watch the ball when so close to their strings, sometimes preferring to have a clearer view of the whole situation on court. They can sometimes afford this liberty because of their exceptionally well grooved strokes. Know about this and try it, if only because it may convince you better than anything else that for lesser mortals the closer you watch the ball the better.

As a match goes along, the ball itself becomes softer and larger. Each hit fractionally lowers its compression and disturbs its cloth cover. You know this and your opponent may not. He may worry that in the third set of a match the balls have become somewhat lighter and more difficult to control. Your attitude is that you will see and control the balls better, because they are larger and softer.

The next thing to concentrate on is to hit the ball over the net—always. You are not giving yourself a chance if your mistakes go half into the net and half out. Hit every ball over. This may sound obvious, but if you watch other people's mistakes you will see it is not obvious to them. To ensure that most of your shots go into court, use ball control. This is where your strings come into the picture.

Long Contact

Hold the ball on your strings. Carry the ball. Follow through the ball. All these phrases add up to long contact. Long contact is mainly in your mind, but is physically there too. The ball will stay in contact with your strings a fraction longer. That is only a small point. The big one is the great difference in mental control you get. Taking, for simplicity, a flat drive, contrast Illus. 6 and 7.

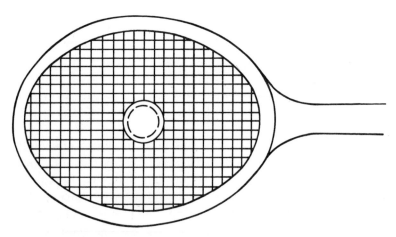

Illus. 6. LONG CONTACT: Flatten the ball against your strings. You can hit hard, but with a feeling of control.

For practice, play forehand after forehand over the net with long contact. At first, particularly if you have flicked at the ball in the past, your long contact forehand will feel rather ponderous. This feeling will improve, through a stage of slight clumsiness, to a satisfactory one of solid determination. You will feel the solid weight of the ball. You will hit firmer and firmer and then more and more heavily, and the ball, unless

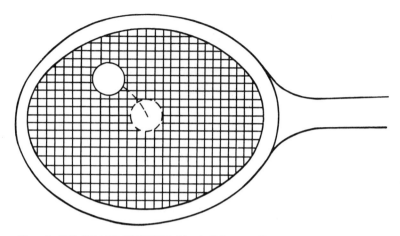

Illus. 7. HIT, BUT NO THOUGHT: The ball jumps off your strings fast but with no feeling of control.

you hit it much too high, will continue to land in court. You will feel that your forehand is your strength, as distinct from your serve (which has to land in a small area) or your backhand (which hasn't as much swing and power).

Sweeping with long contact against a ball that is getting softer and bigger takes care of a host of things. Look back at the previous list. For example, you can forget that your forehand had once gone astray. Co-ordination takes care of itself. You turn well sideways in order to get a long enough swing and this takes care of your footwork. Long contact prevents swinging your body round too soon. You watch the ball well because you now want to—and so on. You can be your own analyst with ease.

Long contact is the basis of your forehand. This is not to ignore getting to the ball quickly and stroking ever more smoothly. Spin comes into it too, but we'll leave spin till later.

Low, High and Rising Balls

If your waist-high forehand is sound, high or low forehands will not worry you. If low balls seem to interfere with your normal stroke, bend your knees more deeply. This brings your waist nearer to the level of the ball—so that you can play more comfortably.

A characteristic of people who are under-confident about playing forehands against high balls is that they start the racket down near waist level and then uncertainly wobble it up to the ball. It makes a world of difference against a high bouncing ball to start your backswing up high.

When you play a rising ball, consciously close your racket face, that is, turn it downwards. Illus. 8 shows by simple geometry the result of leaving the face square to the net.

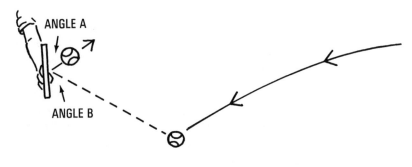

Illus. 8.

3. BACKHAND ADEQUACY

ONE GREAT TROUBLE about having an unsound backhand, if you're right-handed, is that it is a natural target for your opponents, both right- and left-handed. Most right-handers find it easiest to play straight forehands and cross-court backhands, and a typical left-hander pulls his forehand across court and slides his backhand to his off side. All four shots will automatically be directed towards an unsound backhand of a right-hander.

As well, there's the net-rusher. The guiding principle of his tennis life is to play to opponent's backhand and take the net.

You can see that, above all, your backhand needs to be solid. After that, it needs to be as free and flexible as its first requirement, solidity, will allow.

Grip

It is virtually impossible to have a solid backhand stroke with an inadequate backhand grip. Please refer once more to the illustrations of the Extreme Eastern and Eastern forehand grips at Illus. 2 and 3. Get your racket out and make a few backhand swings using these grips as backhand grips. They look like Illus. 9 and, even with no ball to hit against, they feel weak.

Illus. 9. INADEQUATE BACKHAND GRIP: The Extreme Eastern or Eastern forehand grip is weak if used as your backhand grip. The back of the hand faces forward and the wrist is bent.

Now try the Australian forehand grip (Illus. 4), as a backhand grip. It's better, especially if you keep your wrist low, but still not strong enough so you progress to the last forehand grip, the Continental (Illus. 5) and this time you are not disappointed. Meeting the ball about 6 inches or so in front of your right hip (the hip nearer the net as you stand sideways to the net), you have a feeling of strength. Most players prefer to reinforce this feeling by advancing the thumb diagonally across the back of the handle.

This description should be enough. However, please see Illus. 10 for general confirmation. *General only,* keep your own comfortable naturalness.

Illus. 10. ADEQUATE BACKHAND GRIP

Girls and young men may not find this grip strong enough. If so, they should not use it, because for them it is inadequate. For more support they should turn their hands a little farther round, anti-clockwise from the Continental forehand grip. Generally, despite Chris Evert, it is unwise to adopt a two-handed grip, because it restricts your reach. If a young player thinks of doing this as a temporary expedient, it is more likely to become an unchangeable method. In the hands of a star a two-handed grip creates a sensation, but two-handed grips have been tried for over 40 years, if not longer, and have not displaced one-handed play.

For men players the Continental forehand grip, used as a backhand grip, is adequate, particularly if the thumb is advanced across the handle to block-in the gap between forefinger and thumb. Turning your hand farther round, as discussed in the preceding paragraph, will produce yet more strength of grip—but this will then be at the expense of flexibility. This will allow your opponent to hit more balls just a little too far behind your (now stronger but stiffer) grip for your backhand stroke to be able to return them properly. Players whose backhands are weak because of an inadequate grip are obvious prey for net-attackers, but so too are those with stiff backhands.

Altering Your Backhand Grip

Your own correct backhand grip can vary a little to suit your own individual strength and comfort and naturalness. However, if you are certain your present grip is wrong, you should try altering it. Approach this with confidence because there are not the same dangers that beset forehand grip alterations. A backhand follows more defined lines than an individual forehand. You are not so committed to the most natural spot in relation to your body to hit the ball. Your backhand grip is strong in itself (stronger than your forehand grip) so you need less backswing and this makes your timing easier, whether your grip is original or altered.

If your previous backhand grip could have been called inadequate, the new one will always feel stronger and at first a little clumsy. If your previous grip had been one of strength alone, the new one will always feel freer and at first somewhat weak.

Forehand to Backhand Grip Change

If your previous backhand grip was inadequate, at least the change from your forehand grip to reach it was not great. An adequate backhand grip will demand a larger change, meaning you must be quicker. However, you can change grip from forehand to backhand by the time you have taken your racket back, if you know how to do it. Awaiting, say, a service, hold the throat of your racket between your left-hand fingers and the ball of your thumb. If the ball comes to your backhand, take the racket back with your left hand and at the same time twist the throat slightly clockwise with the ball of your thumb. Your grip will have been changed before you swing your racket forward.

This is good news, but do not gild the lily. The facts remain that Continental-forehand-grip players are quicker between forehand and backhand than any other stylists are and that the main disadvantage of the Extreme Eastern grip is its large change to an adequate backhand grip.

Footwork

With an adequate grip, probably the next most important thing is to be sideways to the net when you hit your backhand—in practice, even more than sideways. You can accomplish this with definite footwork, or more accurately, foot placement.

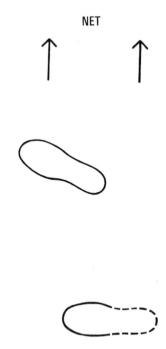

Illus. 11. STEP STRONGLY TO YOUR BACKHAND: Take a good firm step towards the ball with your right foot. Bend your right knee. Head down, lean your right shoulder to the ball.

Whenever you are not crowded close to the ball, step out strongly to it with your right foot, as shown in Illus. 11.

Hitting Outside the Ball

When you were learning to play the backhand you were taught to aim it straight. You were not advised to aim in one direction and then pull across the ball to hit it in another. This would have been confusing and harmful. Now you have been playing for a while and you have a backhand weakness

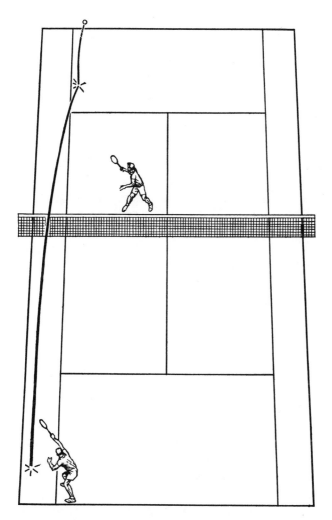

Illus. 12. A DOWN-THE-LINE PASSING SHOT CURVING INWARDS: Hit outside the ball, as for a cross-court shot, and the ball can pass beyond the net player's reach and curve back inside the line.

to overcome. Perhaps you have unknowingly developed a habit of hitting your backhand *inside* the ball.

If this is true, you will be in a vulnerable situation if your opponent plays deep to your backhand and closes in to the net. Lobbing alone is not good enough. You want passing shots— cross-court and down-the-line.

Cross-court

For most people this is an easier backhand to make than down-the-line. (Only those who hit their backhands *inside* the ball prefer hitting to the off rather than cross-court.) A cross-court passing shot mostly demands to be angled and short, as it has to pass across your opposing net man's body and yet land in court. A concept of hitting slightly outside the ball is likely to improve your confidence greatly in making this shot.

Down-the-line

This is the bête noire. Your opponent nearly always seems to cover the ball and volley a winner, or, in getting it out of his reach, you hit the ball into the doubles alley. Solution: having read the preceding paragraph, now look at Illus. 12.

Making the Most of an Inside Backhand

An inside backhand is not suited to making strong passing shots. It may, however, be your only natural way of hitting the ball. You are going to stay with your own stroke, and you want to know how to improve it so you can make a passing shot.

Play it with touch instead of speed. If there is an opening, by all means use more speed. When you cannot pass your opponent outright, keep the ball low and place it as well as you can. Count on getting another chance, another shot to play.

4. SERVICE CONCEPT

THE SCORE is 5-4 to you, last set, your serve. You're serving for set and match. You've only got to serve out the set. *Only?* You'd rather your opponent was serving and then at least he'd be the one who had to avoid any double fault. If so, it is sufficient indication that your serve is a weakness.

Over the Net

The first thing to be clear about is that your serve must go over the net. Getting it in is another story, but it must be free enough to sail over the net. The service is an overhead shot so its tendency is downwards, and it always "wants" to go into the net. Everyone's does.

It is obvious that many servers do not realize any of this. Obsessed with control, they over-control. They go in for excessive topspin and go into contortions applying it. They throw the ball into a position where they cannot hit it hard. And, after all this, their serve finishes in the net—where they may as well have landed it gently underarm. There are also plenty of servers with free and uncomplicated actions who bang their first serves into the net—and falter their second ones into it too.

Relax

If you are tense about your serve you need to relax. Here are three ways:

1. Give up putting too much hope, let alone desperation, into your first service being a winner. Instead, expect it to be returned. Then, you will move to the ball and perhaps be able to attack from there. With this thought—that you would sooner attack your opponent's service-return than receive his service—you will be far from wishing away your serve.

2. Accept the ballistics fact that your serve tends downwards, meaning that it tends to land somewhat shorter than your aim point, and serve for the service line. When the ball goes farther than your aim point, you must have hit it below center on your strings, that is, somewhere between center and the racket's throat.

3. This suggestion is necessarily for a practice session only and is specially recommended if you have a tied-up and hard-working service action. Stand well inside the baseline and serve more simply from there, concentrating only on aiming with long contact. Move back by stages to the baseline—from where the net no longer looks so far away as to justify all the effort your serve previously used to take.

Grip

You may have heard that you *must* use the Continental forehand grip (Illus. 5) for your service, but while this grip is desirable it is not mandatory. A service action is like a throw. However relaxed you make your throw, there is some amount of wrist snap in it—and the Continental grip aids wrist snap in a serve. But if you feel rocky with this grip, serve with your Eastern one. If your wrist is not strong (as is the case with young players and many girls), the Eastern is a better service grip for you than the Continental.

Swerve

Few players use an Extreme Eastern or Western grip and serve with a flat racket face. The great majority of them use Continental or Eastern and serve with some degree of slice. This slice swerves the ball a little, from the server's right to his left. The swerve does not confuse the receiver, so there is no point in slicing heavily for more swerve. You will only lose pace and eventually mis-hit as well.

Nevertheless, the swerve has distinct value. Curving the flight of the ball, even if only by a small amount, gives the ball a longer path to travel after it has crossed the net and so gives it more chance of dropping in court. It adds to your confidence to feel that you are serving/swerving the ball. *Over* the net, of course. Swerve gives the ball a longer path, too, from you *to* the net, and so is another factor in the ball's tendency to land in the net. You have to swerve it over and, from there on, the swerve is acting *for* you. Do not overdo it, or you will develop a freak service and eventually find yourself in need of Relaxation Three therapy above.

Throw

The most common mistake made by beginners is to throw the ball too low, but many medium-grade players throw it too far forward. Admittedly this equates with freedom, and we do see champions throwing the ball well forward and leaning and hitting into it with a grand mixture of superb confidence, great speed and swift advance to the net. Lesser players—poor servers, not good ones—may get the freedom part but that is about all. A throw too far forward causes them to hit their full-speed first serves into the net and stumble anxiously forward with their second ones.

The calm type of server who can always send his second ball well clear of the net and in, and who never seems to mind how much delay there may be between his first and second serves, will always be found to throw the ball less forward. His mechanical advantage is that he is in good balance. This leads to a norm of successful serves, and this gives him confidence. He would never prefer his opponent to be serving.

Once again, be aware of this but don't overdo it.

If you have any difficulty in throwing the ball exactly where you want to, check yourself for two points. First: you should hold the ball between the ball of your thumb and a point above the first joints of your forefinger and middle finger. This gives you the best feel of it. Second: you should not release it from low down and thus make a long throw. Release the ball above your shoulder. Watch other good servers.

These two points contribute more towards making a good throw than would holding only one ball in your hand. With one ball you either fumble about for the second ball, or else play the rest of the rally with it jammed in your pocket, or you have to throw it away. Two-handers, of necessity, get involved in all this, but a single-handed player shouldn't.

Pairs of Serves

The weakness in service most castigated by coaches and tennis writers alike consists of a cannonball first serve that rarely goes even close, and a lollypop second ball. Obviously, it is better to make the two serves nearer to one speed and to get a lot of first serves in. Once again, however, some players overdo things and serve the first ball in such an agony of caution that it is weak and short, and sometimes even in the net (which it hardly disturbs).

There are two kinds of *good* pairs of serves. One is where the two serves are basically alike except for ball speed, and the other consists of a strong first serve backed by a reliable kick or topspin second serve. Both concepts are sound.

The two-similar-serves concept presumes both serves being alike in service action and the spot the ball is thrown to. The speed of action is also similar, meaning that for both serves you hit *at* the ball at about the same racket speed. The only difference is that for the second ball you use a little more spin and swerve so that the ball can have a safer (higher) net clearance and yet land in court. The speed of this second ball is, of course, somewhat reduced.

The result is that you will get a lot of first serves in and those that miss will be excellent sighters for the following second ball.

The system is not meant to be inflexible. On your good days you can increase the speed of your first ball. However, if it's your good day, no doubt you will speed up the second one too. In any event this concept builds your confidence. It makes you groove your service action and feel purposeful—in contrast with having a nondescript first serve that you hope will go in, and another type of nondescript second serve that you fear won't go in.

Finally, this type of good pair serving is relaxed. It fits in with your game plan. True, you must expect most balls to be returned to you, but not necessarily aggressively, so that you can attack from there.

The concept of the strong first serve backed by the reliable kicker that arcs high over the net and drops steeply and safely into court is basically dependent on that kick serve being reliable. So the idea is really that you develop a specialist second serve—and then you will be free to frighten the life out of your opponent with your first.

For a topspin serve, throw the ball a little farther back than usual and more to the left—about above your head. To roll on topspin, your racket must be rising as it hits the ball, ending its swing to the right of your right leg. To serve a kicker, throw the ball farther again to your left, as this makes you whip your racket up more sharply—giving more topspin and a kick on bouncing. The good point about any topspin shot is that once the ball is safely over the net it is likely to drop in. The bad point is that the more topspin you try for the greater is the chance of a mis-hit.

Renowned servers mostly use a fast first serve and a strong topspin or kicking second. So, too, do the best servers in lesser grades. You may become one of them.

Whatever else this section may have done, at least it alerts you to regard your serve as a pair of serves. Realization alone is often the first step in overcoming a weakness.

Watching the Ball

You do this by keeping your head up until you have hit the ball. Champions do not keep their heads up all the time. Their grooved swings can permit them to lower their heads a little earlier for better rhythm. Sunday afternoon players don't keep their heads up either, but here it's ignorance and not rhythm.

When you serve the ball *over* the net and it goes out, it is because you did not hit the center of your strings and instead hit somewhat below it. And you did this because you did not keep your head up to watch the ball.

Long Contact?

Yes, most certainly you should use it. Long contact improves every shot you have time to use it with. There is a bonus, too. In taking this time you won't be hurrying your serve: a basic principle.

5. VOLLEYING

VOLLEYING is not the average player's weakness. There are a few good reasons why not. You play your volleys from nearer the net than your groundstrokes, from where it is easier to hit the ball into court. The approaching ball does not change its direction as much as when it bounces before you hit a groundstroke. A ball is easier to hit on the fly than on the bounce.

The volley takes only a short stroke, so it is comparatively easy to time the ball, to meet it at the desired spot in front of your body, and to hit it with the center of the strings.

How can volleying be anyone's weakness? There are two extreme cases: if your eyesight changes focus abnormally slowly, or if you become so set in your service and groundstroke rhythms that you become paralyzed by a ball on the fly. Apart from these two cases, volleying can be only a comparative weakness. Your volleying may not be as good as other players of your standard or it may not be as good as your groundstrokes are, by comparison. However, practically everyone can make a one-shot volley more easily than a groundstroke.

The first step in overcoming a general volleying weakness is to convince yourself of all this by trial on the court.

Watching the Ball

Many people watch the ball properly for groundstrokes and not for volleys. They imagine the speed of a volley to be far greater than it is. They don't watch the ball the whole way and so have only a blurred sight of it during its last few yards, or even feet. Then they snatch at it. This snatch they imagine to be correct form, for everyone knows, don't they, that you musn't swing at a volley? You punch it or block it.

If you watch the ball calmly, your jab will have a fair chance of being the punch or block you want it to be.

Meeting the Ball

As a general rule for all types of volleys (meaning waist-high, high or low) you should meet the ball farther in front of you (farther in front of whichever hip is pointed nearer to the net) than you do with your groundstrokes. This gives you a better sight of the ball and allows more rigidity in your grip. Overdoing this will put you out of balance, which you will easily recognize.

Grip

Like the service, the Continental grip is not mandatory. Its advantage in serving is that it allows more wrist snap. Its main advantage in volleying is that in rapid-fire exchanges you can be quicker between forehand and backhand. Other advantages are that it is easier for low volleying, and that it gives you greater reach for a wide ball.

Please note that none are advantages at all if you do not feel confident when volleying with a Continental grip. Volley with your Eastern grip if you feel more at home that way—you will be less dextrous but stronger, and overall more effective.

You may be a player who takes little or no notice of grip. On the other hand, you may be in the opposite category. You may have read a convincing book, such as one by the great Tilden, that tells you to drive Eastern but volley Continental. For you, this could be a case of a book's doing a player more harm than good. Try things, experiment—but settle for what feels most *effective*. You won't be wrong.

On this tack of possible misunderstandings, perhaps you are among the people who have misunderstood the volleying tenet, "Keep your racket head up." This is intended to mean that you should not let your racket head drop, but instead keep it at least in line with your wrist or slightly above it. Not understanding, some players volley with the racket head way up, making a sharp angle between handle and arm. This makes them unnatural and cramped, with a resultingly weak volley.

High Volleys

These can hardly be anyone's weakness. The easiest place to hit them is into the large court in front of you. A good way of looking at it is that this area is bigger than the net and the space between the lines and the fences. However, always remember to turn well sideways, or you may needlessly angle the ball too much and hit it over the sideline.

Low Volleys

In contrast to a high volley, the easiest place to hit a low volley is into the net. Against a fast shot, your low volley may clear the net and sail beyond the baseline. To low volley well you need technique and touch.

TECHNIQUE. Because waist-high volleying is easy and natural, the soundest low-volleying technique is to take your waist down to the ball's level, as far as you comfortably can. The way you do this is to bend your knees. Be prepared to bend them deeply, if necessary right down to a squatting position. It is no use bending your back, because then you will lose your balance. (See Illus. 13 on the next page.)

Bringing your waist down to the ball means that you can play your stroke in a normal manner, namely with the racket head

Illus. 13. LOW VOLLEYING TECHNIQUE: Bring your waist down to the ball, back straight, knees bent.

in line with your wrist or a little above. You will not need to drop your racket head—and it is now time to understand why this is poor form.

Contrast your normal more-or-less-horizontal racket with a vertical one, that is, with the head down by your ankle. Your object is to send the ball somewhere from 3 to 6 inches over the net. With a horizontal racket, a slight difference in timing and meeting the ball will not vary the height of your shot by much. In other words, you have a safe margin for error. By contrast, if you are late in your timing with a vertical racket, the ball will go well down into the net, and if you are early it will be way up in the air.

Another thing is that the nearer the ball is to your eye-level, the better you can see it. You cannot take your eye-level right down to the ball, but, in playing with well-bent knees and a horizontal racket, the difference in levels is far less than if you stand up straight and play a low ball with a vertical racket.

A dropped racket head is not necessarily as extreme as a vertical racket, but it's on the way there.

TOUCH. You may not want to be a touch player, preferring to be a robust hitter, stroking strongly whenever you can. Be that as it may, every type of player needs some degree of touch when volleying a fast ball that is below net height. Unless you absorb some of the ball's speed, your low volley will send the ball fast into the net or fast over the net and over the line as well.

Once you know that you must absorb some of the speed, you can do it. As an aid, hold the racket handle more in your fingers. This is not a weak grip, using only your fingers, but it feels very different from holding the racket hard against the butt of your hand in a grip of iron. You will learn for yourself, better than anyone can try to explain to you, the feeling of touch and control you get when your fingers are involved.

Easier Said Than Done?

Volleying is easier said than done to the extent that it is one thing to volley balls that a practice partner is feeding to you, and another to be in the right place to play a volley in a set or match against an opponent who is trying to pass you. With high and waist-high volleys, however, you will find there is not much difference between practicing and playing a set. It is low volleying that proves your worth.

A Tiger at the Net

As an example of low volleying being a severe test, take the average net tiger. This type of volleyer charges close up to the net and disposes of any weak returns he may have forced. In doubles, he intercepts strongly against tentative service returns.

It is good play as far as it goes but unless his low volleying is also good this type of player quickly folds up into a paper tiger. High volleying and agility are not enough to make a true volleyer.

A Hard Man to Pass

This is the man who can be called a volleyer. Secure at all points, he does not need to crowd too closely to the net (where you can easily lob over him) in order to avoid a low volley. He takes as many balls as possible close to the net and high above it, but he closes in only after he has assessed your shot. If you play the ball low, he can handle a low volley. If you lob, his position is far enough back to cover it. Similarly his position gives him more time to cover your attempted passing shots. He's always there. He becomes known as a hard man to pass.

He has, of course, another thing going for him: anticipation. (We'll come to that in due course.) Meanwhile, he would never have developed into the type he is without his low-volleying confidence.

6. HALF-VOLLEY, LOB, SMASH
AND LEFT-HANDED WEAKNESSES

A GENUINE HALF-VOLLEY is not a difficult stroke. What you really want to avoid is playing your half-volley hesitantly late, so it becomes a stroke that is about three-quarters half-volley and one-quarter rising ball. Successful half-volleying is playing the ball as closely as possible to its point of impact with the court. Whenever you can do this, a half-volley becomes easier to play than a very low volley. There is less strain on your wrist and you are not so likely to hit the ball into the net.

Whether a half-volley is an easy close-to-the-ground type or a difficult one, the best technique is similar to that for low volleying: bend your knees deeply to bring your waist down to the ball, and then play with a horizontal racket. But don't necessarily block the ball as you do with a volley. Instead, after a very short backswing, follow through strongly with covering topspin. This latter is an integral part of the stroke because you play the ball with a closed racket face. (Refer to Illus. 8, concerning forehand rising-ball play.)

Weak Lobs

Many players seem to have a blind spot in the matter of lobbing. They seldom mis-hit the ball and successfully send it up in the air in the shape of a lob, but too short. It meets its just fate and ten minutes later they do the same thing again.

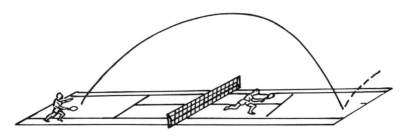

Illus. 14. AIMING A LOB: B is the aiming point instead of C. AB is only about half the distance AC. Also, since you hit a lob upward, your aiming point is more in line with this.

It is a paradox that anyone tends to lob short, when you consider that the lob is the only shot in tennis that is sometimes better hit out than hit weakly into play. A pitifully short lob is soul-destroying. If there are onlookers, you feel ashamed of yourself, and you are likely to feel self-conscious over the next point as well. If your lob does go out, your net opponent may have been forced to turn round and chase it hard. It is then you, not he, who has more confidence in the next point to be played.

For some players this little homily may be enough, but you may demand more assistance in playing the stroke. After all, a lob is not easily aimed—no one balloons anything he wants to aim. Also a lob has to be played a long way, from baseline to baseline.

You may like to try halving this distance. Instead of aiming to land the ball near the opposing back line (which is hardly aiming it anyway) aim the ball to its highest point. (See Illus. 14.)

This method of lobbing is mechanical rather than natural, so don't be surprised if you find it difficult. Try it out to see if it suits you, and even if you finally discard it, you will have learned something about lobbing meanwhile.

Smash

It sounds wrong to call anyone's smash a weakness if half his trouble is that he hits it too hard. However, in terms of winning points, it is certainly a weakness. Worse, it exchanges a winning position for a lost one.

In remedying your smash, you might like to know that the smash is prone to a more constant error than any other shot: more than seven out of ten missed smashes go into the net, *not* out. This statistic goes back a long way—before the mighty Bill Tilden's time in the 1920's, because he quoted it. Observe this constant error for yourself and thereafter be fully conscious of it. Against a deep lob, aim the ball *over* the net, *well* over it.

When a smash does go out it is usually a long way out, after a somewhat upward flight of the ball. You will realize this is really a form of mis-hit, but not a wood mis-hit. The strings hit the ball, from *below* their center. So, hit with the center of your strings and aim the ball over the net. The ball aims itself downwards.

If you are not confident with your smash, no doubt your greatest worry is timing a high or deep lob. It is likely that your present method is to wait a reasonable time for the ball and then rather hurriedly go into your full service action. The reason? You have heard and even seen in print that your smash should be identical with your serve. The fact is that your smash *should* be highly similar to your serve (you will naturally make it that way), but it should not be identical. The circumstances are different, so your smash becomes a slightly modified serve. You do not need as much action. In a few words: to serve, take your racket up behind your back; to smash, take it up in front of your body.

Waiting for the ball, hold your racket ready by your shoulder. To poise yourself, put your left hand up to the ball. (See Illus. 15 on the next page.)

Illus. 15. SET TO SMASH: Ready your racket and steady your left hand.

For the final moment of timing, most good players rise into the air to meet the ball. Try it. It prevents your having that terrible feeling that the ball is falling down on top of you and that it, rather than you, dictates the last fraction of timing. If you feel safer on the ground, stay there, because the main feeling you need while smashing is safety. The inherent speed of a smash is all the speed you need.

Left-handers

This section is *for* left-handers, as distinct from playing against left-handers.

Typical left-handed weaknesses are a literally weak backhand, erratic volleying and predictable direction with overhead strokes. Let's assume you are a "typical" left-hander.

Your weak backhand stems from learning tennis by playing doubles with right-handed partners, always from the left court. You found you could play almost every service return with your forehand and so you came to use a most effective grip for this, provided you were not worrying much about your backhand. This is the Extreme Eastern. As explained in Chapter 1, this grip needs the largest change of grip if you are to have an adequate backhand grip. The typical left-hander uses only an inadequate backhand grip.

To avoid the opposing net man in doubles a left-hander must hit a backhand return of service to his off side. A typical left-hander does this, with his inadequate backhand grip, by raising his elbow, dropping the racket head, and hitting noticeably inside the ball. Such a backhand is a poor substitute for the type of backhand described in Chapter 3, particularly the section "Hitting Outside the Ball." Also refer to Illus. 12. The pity is that this lesser backhand becomes the left-hander's most natural one.

Do not alter your forehand (certain to be a strong shot) or its grip. Instead practice changing grip far more quickly so that you can use a more adequate backhand grip. Play all your doubles practice sets from the right court if you can. Practice a cross-court backhand with a lowered wrist, instead of a raised elbow. Play in the left court when you play a match, because it is the basis of tactics to be using your best shot, your forehand, as much as possible.

The reason for your volleying being erratic is that your

forehand and backhand volleys are less of a pair than a right-hander's. You tend to take a longer swing on the forehand side, and to have that raised-elbow, dropped-racket-head type of stroke for your backhand volleys.

Your predictable overhead (service and smash) direction is to your offside, that is, towards a right-hander's forehand corner. Reason? You learned to serve from the first side, from which a right-hander learns a curve but a left-hander to send the ball away to his off. As time goes by, a right-hander varies his direction more than a typical left-hander seems to.

Unrealized weaknesses pointed out are halfway cured. The other half is up to you. If you are a typical left-hander you are not lacking in self-reliance.

7. SPIN

SPIN MAY BE A WEAKNESS of yours in any of at least three ways:

- You are vulnerable to its use by an opponent.

- You do not use it to advantage and limit both your effectiveness and your stroke range.

- You overdo it.

To overcome these weaknesses you need a thorough understanding of spin. Partial knowledge is not much good. It often means you need to think things out when you've no time to.

Perhaps the first thing to understand about spin is that to some degree it is on every one of your shots. A cannonball serve may be called flat, but usually there is some fraction of slice or twist to it. Even where there is not, the action of the racket strings coming over the ball puts a trace of forward roll on the ball. Take out your racket, hold it in a Continental grip, go through the action of a flat service, and you will see what I mean.

Similarly, a so-called flat drive is only comparatively flat. Follow the action of a flat drive slowly through with your racket and notice that, although the racket may meet the ball flat, it begins to rise in its forward swing before the ball has left the strings. Thus, some amount of forward spin has been imparted to the ball.

If you have been somewhat unsure about spin, it may make you feel more at home to know that there is some degree of it on all your usual shots. However, you can see that "spin" really means "deliberately applied spin."

Two Families

The two large families are Topspin and Underspin. It would be more suitable if we called them Overspin and Underspin, and kept the term "topspin" to mean, say, a medium amount of overspin. However, for every time you hear anyone say "overspin" you'll hear "topspin" used a dozen times or more, so we will keep to common usage. In this discussion, we will assume that the spin is being applied with a right-handed forehand.

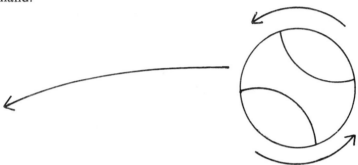

Illus. 16. TOPSPIN: When the ball spins forward its upper half bites into the air, so that the ball must curve downwards in its forward line of flight. This makes it difficult to volley.

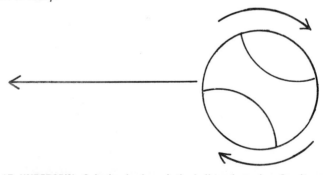

Illus. 17. UNDERSPIN: Spinning backward, the ball tends to rise. Gravity acts in the opposite direction so the ball travels in a fairly straight line above the ground. This makes it easy to volley.

Topspin

Since topspin is used to cover all degrees of topspin, for clarity in your mind you may like to apply some suitable names to the various degrees: A small amount of intentioned topspin is FORWARD SPIN. A little more you may call ROLL. More, just TOPSPIN. Still more, HEAVY TOPSPIN. Any more spin than that would at best be EXCESSIVE TOPSPIN, but more likely MIS-HIT.

You can apply topspin by hitting slightly below the center of the ball or slightly above center. Driving from behind the baseline, you feel you are hitting slightly below the center of the ball and lifting on the spin. For a ball landing in the service court and bouncing higher than the net, you should feel you are hitting slightly above center and making the ball spin downwards. In either case the direction of the spin and its axis are the same. (See Illus. 18.)

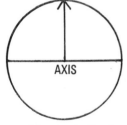

Illus. 18. TOPSPIN, VIEWED FROM THE BACK: Because the ball drops steeply, its bounce is higher than that of a flat drive. Also this height and the forward spin on the ball combine to make the bounce longer.

If you drive cross-court and hit slightly outside the ball, the spin is largely topspin, but there is also a small component of outside sidespin. (See Illus. 19.)

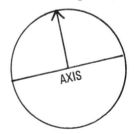

Illus. 19. TOPSPIN, HITTING SLIGHTLY OUTSIDE THE BALL: The main effect is the topspin curve downward and the high and long bounce. The smaller outside spin effect on both curve and bounce is referred to as "going away."

Topspin gives you a double form of ball control: the downward curve of the ball (Illus. 16) and also the long contact that results from rolling the ball a fraction across the short strings before it leaves your racket. (See Illus. 20.)

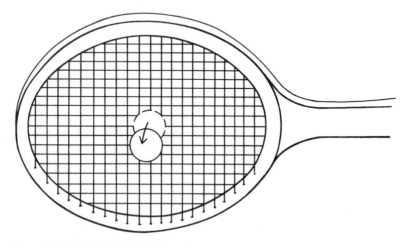

Illus. 20. TOPSPIN CONTACT: This gives the ball both topspin and long contact with your strings.

Underspin

DEMONSTRATION 1. Stand sideways to an imaginary net and hold a ball out at full arm's length (your arm being parallel to the net) about opposite your left (front) hip. Most players tend to use a Continental grip for their underspin strokes, but by all means use an Eastern one if you like. Starting from somewhere above ball height, make (slowly) a short cutting stroke under the ball's surface. This will give the ball pure underspin, or backspin. (See Illus. 21.)

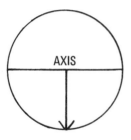

Illus. 21. BACKSPIN: This is pure underspin. The ball hangs in the air. Its bounce is lower and slower than that of a flat drive and, expectedly, more upright.

The small stroke you used was a CUT. If you make it longer and more flowing it will be a SLICE. If you hit at a steeper angle down to the ball, and hence more vigorously, it is a CHOP. This shot is heavily spun. Topspin drives are usually only called topspin drives, but the three underspin shots are generally known by these different names. There is a fourth name: CHIP. This term is used for a cut taken en route to the net. The stroke's full name is CHIP APPROACH SHOT.

DEMONSTRATION 2. Hold the ball out at arm's length and hip height again, and this time hit under and slightly outside it. The resulting spin is shown in Illus. 22.

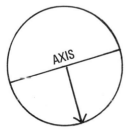

Illus. 22. OUTSIDE UNDERSPIN: This is how most cuts, slices and chops are made. The ball's flight and bounce are similar to those shown in Illus. 21.

DEMONSTRATION 3. Hold the ball out at head height or so, as though it had bounced high. Now slice down and round it. The resulting spin is again outside underspin, but it is referred to as SIDESPIN because this shot has a greater sidespin component than any other normally-made forehand.

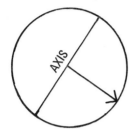

Illus. 23. SIDESPIN: The ball curves widely towards your opponent's right, similar to a slice service. Its bounce breaks slightly in the same direction, again lower and slower than that of a flat drive.

DEMONSTRATION 4. Hold the ball out at knee level and hit slightly under and inside it. This gives inside underspin and the stroke is really a slice. However, because this shot is usually made as a long stroke with little spin it is referred to as an UNDERSPIN DRIVE. Thus we have a fifth recognized name for an underspin shot. There may be very little inside spin or underspin on the ball, but any degree of either affects the action of the ball and differentiates this stroke from a flat drive.

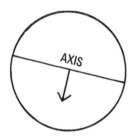

Illus. 24. UNDERSPIN DRIVE: Slightly, but perceptibly in comparison with a flat drive the ball hangs in the air and swings to your opponent's left. The bounce is also slower and lower.

Ball Control with Underspin Shots

The demonstrations and illustrations have shown that in all underspin shots the ball spins backwards to some extent. Referring to Illus. 17, this means the ball tends to sail out of court. Yet you know that the cut, for instance, is a ball-control shot, often seen used as a safe mark-time stroke against a fast drive. How is this reconciled?

In the first place, a cut is easily made. It needs only a short swing, so little can go wrong with your timing in meeting a fast ball. Secondly (and this applies to all underspin strokes), you have a form of long contact. (See Illus. 25, which is similar to Illus. 20.)

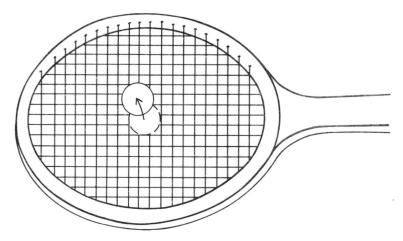

Illus. 25. UNDERSPIN CONTACT: The ball slides a fraction up the short strings before leaving them, giving you long contact.

Using Underspin Shots

In general, underspin strokes lift the ball more easily over the net. The cut can be used for a mark-time shot, as we have seen. Caught off balance, you can use it to recover quickly. When you haven't time to drive, you can slice the ball, should you want to do rather more with your stroke than defensively cut it. You can slow the game down with slices. You can also slice round the ball when it is too wide for you to get behind it and drive. The chop, along with other excessive forms of spin, has largely disappeared from tennis. It used to be feared for its disconcerting bounce, particularly on grass courts soon after rain, and no doubt it was a terror to the lady players of the day.

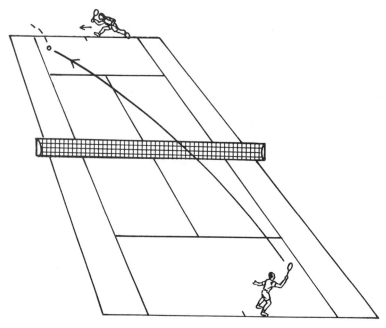

Illus. 26. DOWNWARD SLICE, BASELINE PENETRATION: Both curve and bounce are "going away."

A chip approach shot allows you to play a quickly made stroke and advance to the net quickly to take up a good position. At the same time, the ball does not reach your opponent soon enough for him to pass you before you have gained your desired net position. Stated another way: If you drove the ball, you would take longer in making your shot and getting to your net position; also your faster drive would reach your opponent sooner. As a result, he would be attempting his passing shot before you had gained a good net position.

The downward slice, with its sidespin and strong curve, can be a useful shot on suitable occasions. (See Illus. 26 and 27.)

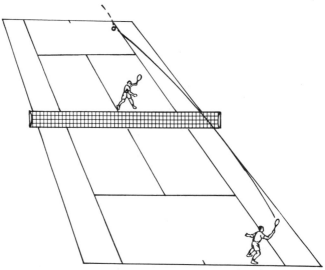

Illus. 27. DOWNWARD SLICE, DOWN-THE-LINE PASSING SHOT: The ball can be hit beyond the netman's reach, curving into court. See Illus. 12 again.

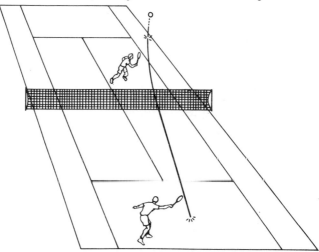

Illus. 28. UNDERSPIN DRIVE, DOWN-THE-LINE PASSING SHOT: Out of reach, but out of court.

The underspin drive mostly fails as a passing shot. (See Illus. 28.) Here a topspin shot should have been used.

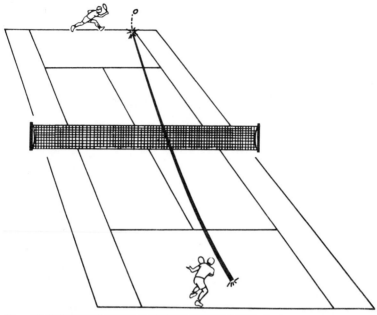

Illus. 29. UNDERSPIN DRIVE, BASELINE PENETRATION: Both swerve and bounce are going away.

However, it has baseline penetration. (See Illus. 29.)

Summarizing the use of forehand underspin, a few general principles will have become clear:

■ Underspin provides an easy way to lift low balls clear of the net.

■ Underspin strokes are steady and safe (and may sometimes be penetrating) against an opponent at the baseline.

■ The chip, holding the ball in the air longer, makes time for you as a useful net-approach shot.

■ Underspin strokes fail against net play. They sail more or less straight at no great speed and are easy to volley. Because they do not dip they are likely to miss the sideline, particularly when hit from net height or lower. Swerve from inside spin worsens this tendency. The downward slice can be used as shown in Illus. 27, but only if hit fast enough to elude the net man.

No one should base his forehand on underspin. It is too vulnerable to a volleying attack. Even an opponent who is normally a baseliner will come to the net and feed on it.

It may appear sound policy to cut and slice steadily while your opponent is at the baseline, and to pass him with flat or topspin drives whenever he takes the net. In practice, however, a few difficulties arise. Your cuts and slices, and their bounces too, will be slower than his strokes, so that you put him under little pressure and may even play him into form. This means he will probably be able to beat you from the baseline alone. When he does take the net, you will probably not be confident in changing from your easily-made cuts or slices to drives that are more exacting in execution.

You should, instead, follow the pattern set by hundreds of good players and dozens of champions: base your forehand on flat and topspin driving, supplemented by underspin strokes as called for. *That* is the way to develop a wide range of strokes.

Topspin Again

Disenchanted with underspin and even its part in stroke range, by now you may have decided to concentrate on topspin alone. If it gives you double ball control from the baseline and is best for angling past a net man, and also makes the most difficult shot to volley, you may wonder why you should bother with anything else.

Here is the other side, which you should take into account. It is easy to become obsessed with topspin. This causes you to apply it more and more. You have been previously warned that this in turn leads to mis-hitting the ball. Moreover, you may find yourself working a lot harder than you need to, grinding on topspin when a flat drive would be much easier to play. Many topspin players often land the ball short, from which point their opponents take charge of the rally. A topspin-only concept tends to draw you away from the basic principle of aiming directly. Topspin brings the ball down all right, but true ball control is landing the ball exactly where you want to. Experiment on the court will soon convince you that the more spin of any type you put on the ball, topspin included, the less certain you can be of where the ball will land.

These arguments apply more strongly again if you imagine you want to be a master of spin and use a large amount of it in one form or another on every forehand you play. You may reach this decision because you dislike playing against spin yourself. This discussion of spin should have made clear to you the realization that your opponent's game, if it's full of spin, carries its own difficulties and disadvantages, and is not as awesome as you may have once thought. A true master of spin is a player who has spin at his command, but whose game is not solely reliant on it.

Finally, in this section on forehand spin, you may decide you will be a true master of spin one day, but that that day is a long way off and meanwhile you want to settle for utter simplicity. If you want one general all-purpose forehand as your basis, you should settle for the medium-rolled topspin forehand, taken just after the top of the bounce, where the ball is at its slowest in relation to the path of your racket's swing.

Backhand Spin

You cannot fail to have noticed that many good players, and champions too, slice their backhands. This seems to make nonsense of all the disadvantages of forehand spin we have discussed above. However, this is not necessarily so.

In itself, a flat or topspin backhand is a better shot than one made with underspin, but, when taken in conjunction with a player's forehand, it may be more effective to slice the backhand. Against fast serving, players have found they don't have enough time to drive their service returns on both forehand and backhand, so they make do on the backhand side with a more quickly made slice. This slice then becomes their stock backhand for all occasions.

In addition, your backhand grip is stronger than your forehand grip so that you have more power on that side for a shot made with only a short swing. To really worry a net man with a sliced shot, you need accuracy and change of pace. The stronger backhand grip makes these more available from a backhand slice than a forehand one.

Briefly and in general, a player who topspins his forehand and slices his backhand has better balanced strength than one who does the opposite.

Service Spin

No one can volley your serve, so there is no basic objection to slicing a serve. Both slice and topspin serves are aided in landing in court, once they have safely cleared the net, by the spin they carry. The sliced spin makes the ball curve in the air giving it a longer, and hence safer, path to travel before it strikes the court. The topspin on the topspin serve makes it drop sharply.

Notice that the main result of both spins applies to the ball's path in the air, rather than to its bounce after landing. Some artificial surfaces do affect the bounce. For instance, carpet on an indoor court can assist spin to the extent that the going-away bounce of a sliced service can be disconcerting. A concrete surface can make a topspin serve bounce too high for comfort. However, in normal circumstances, excessive slicing usually makes a slice service less effective, and excessive topspin tends to make such a service all kick and no speed.

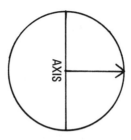

Illus. 30. PURE SLICE SERVICE SPIN: This would involve throwing the ball wide out to the side and so is more theoretical than real. However, it would give maximum curve in the air and break on bouncing, both going away.

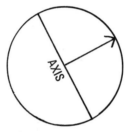

Illus. 31. PRACTICAL SLICE SERVICE SPIN: This has some component of topspin in it. This is one reason why your slice serve tends to go down into the net. The other is the downward action of most serves.

In serving, slice equates with accuracy in placement, and topspin with safe net clearance.

Illus. 30-32 analyze service spin.

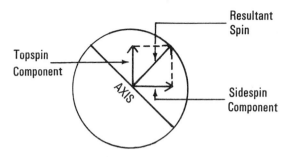

Illus. 32. KICK SERVICE SPIN: The sidespin component makes the ball curve to your opponent's right in the manner of a slice serve. The topspin component makes it drop sharply and bounce high and long. The direction of the resultant spin makes the bounce break back to the receiver's left, that is, bounce is opposite to curve.

Volleying Spin

Underspin is mostly used. It helps lift low volleys, it gives a measure of long contact when you have little or no time to think of it, and it fits in with strokes with little swing, like volleys.

Spin on Lobs

Here underspin equates with safety and topspin with attack— for good players. With lesser performers, underspin often tends to make their lobs shorter than ever while their topspin lobs are more a matter of chance than attack. When using underspin, it is essential to hit firmly. To learn a topspin lob, hit the ball with a slow and deliberate swing and put heavy topspin on it. Master this before attempting an action that is less revealing of your intention.

Smashes

You will remember that unless you have mis-hit below center, seven or more of every ten missed smashes go down

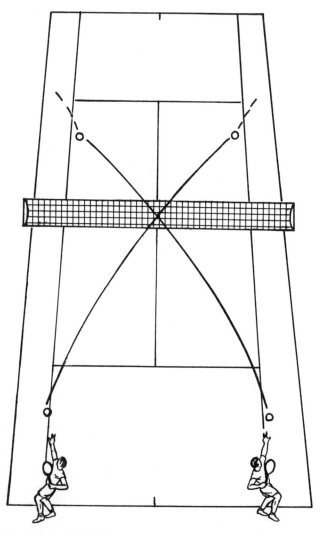

Illus. 33. RIGHT- AND LEFT-HANDERS' SLICE SERVICES: Serving from the widest angle available a right-hander can probably curve the ball as acutely as a left-hander can.

into the net. The smash has a stronger downward tendency than any other stroke. This downward tendency is a form of control, so that spin does not play an important part in smashing.

You may, of course, slice round a smash to angle it, but in handling a high lob you will feel safer in playing with a full-faced racket mainly, rather than attempting to use much spin.

Left-handed Spin

Most people believe a left-hander capable of developing more spin and curve than a right-hander. It seems that way, but it is doubtful if a left-hander really does. For example, see Illus. 33.

One reason a right-handed receiver will feel a greater effect from the left-hander's service curve is that it goes wide of his backhand side. Another reason is that it is in the opposite direction from normal.

Left-handers as a rule use spin more often than do right-handers. Rather than drive flat or with slight roll on forehand and backhand, they usually topspin their forehands strongly and slice or cut inside their backhands. As for service, finding that their left-handed spin often bamboozles an opponent, they go in for it more. Having learned to serve from the first court (which means hitting to the off side), most left-handers serve with a topspin action, but a number specialize in a sharply sliced serve to the left court. This goes wide of the opponent's backhand and, on bouncing, breaks that way as well.

With the information in this chapter you should experiment on the court and become your own analyst. After that, spin will have few secrets for you and you can play it and react to it without thought.

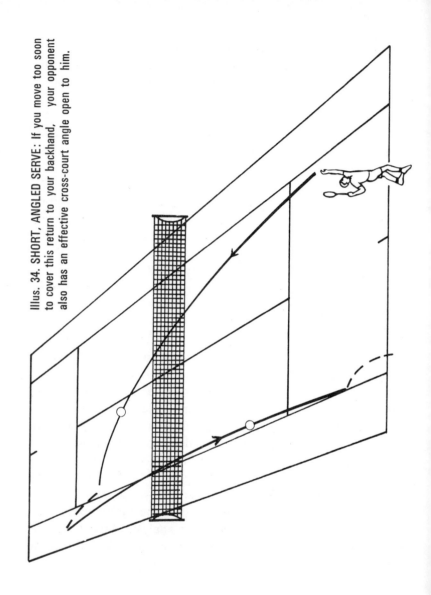

Illus. 34. SHORT, ANGLED SERVE: If you move too soon to cover this return to your backhand, your opponent also has an effective cross-court angle open to him.

8. PLAYING YOUR GAME AND ANTICIPATING YOUR OPPONENT'S

IF YOU ARE NOT SURE whether you use your strokes to best advantage or not, it is long odds that you don't. One type who does use them well is the player who does nothing outstanding in his game, yet is known far and wide as a very hard man to beat. Another is the local champion with his fast serve and other strong shots that everyone admires. Believe me, he too knows how to use his strokes, or he wouldn't be local champion. If you don't know how to use your strokes it is a big weakness in your game.

Service

Serve deep. Make the service line, with a distinct backhand preference, your basic aiming point rather than the more tempting sideline. An inexperienced player feels he may fault and double-fault if he aims deep to the service line, yet, irrationally, he has no qualms about going for an ace near the sideline.

If you serve wide and do not take your opponent by surprise, you lay yourself open. All you will have done, in effect, is to give him a short forehand higher than the net from which he can attack you as shown in Illus. 34. This situation is more dangerous in the right court, particularly if you try to get a better angle by serving well out from the center mark.

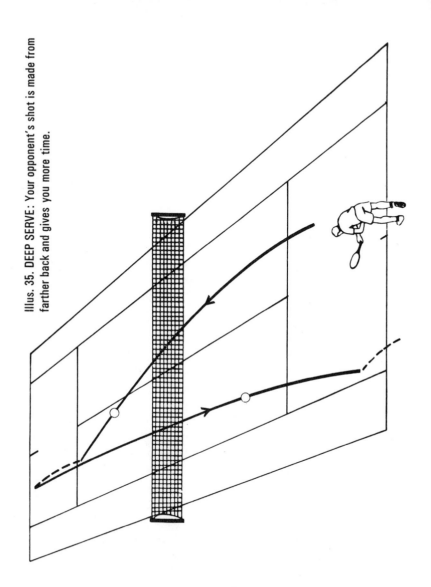

Illus. 35. DEEP SERVE: Your opponent's shot is made from farther back and gives you more time.

Serving from near the center mark and landing the ball within about 18 inches of the service line are better ways to use your service. (See Illus. 35.)

If you want to follow a service to the net, decide to do it before you serve. This makes for a smoother and more balanced net advance.

Return of Service

Preparing to receive a first serve, your mental aim is to be quick, so that you will get the ball back somehow. Normally this is no time to be thinking of playing a long-swinging drive.

Against a second serve, your object is to take over. Return the ball deep, and in most cases you will take over. At least you will have nullified the server's advantage.

Rallying

Don't skim the ball low over the net—it will be short. Hitting well over the net is not playing a beginner's game, as you may have thought. When sitting in the stands above and behind the court, you receive an impression that good players drive every ball low, but if you sit to one side at court level you will see the ball clearing the net by four feet and sometimes more.

Don't play straight back to your opponent—it lets him feel settled. Use both deep corners, or else, perhaps, work more and more to his backhand and then try cross-court. He will have more trouble with his forehand if you don't allow him to play it placidly.

If your opponent shows no inclination to take the net, it is probably because he is under-confident there. Play a few short shots to bring him in and you may find he is no volleyer. Such players are usually easy to lob over too.

Lob

In most cases aim over your opponent's backhand, where he has less reach. After your first weak lob, promise to support a deserving charity if you lob short again the rest of the day.

Approach Shot

Only where your opponent's forehand is hopeless should you direct many approach shots to that side. Normally his forehand is better than that, so make your approach shots to his backhand side. This applies even when your opponent's backhand is his better shot. People are capable of much more with their forehand. It is freer and faster and its direction can be changed later. It may not be as safe as a player's backhand, but it can be more dangerous as a passing shot.

Do not approach from a ball that has landed deep in your court. Your shot will be long and you will give your opponent too much time.

Coming to the Net

Don't come in so far that you can easily be lobbed over. Keep a roof over your house. Sometimes make your advance in two stages, starting with a first volley from about the service line (hit it deep) and a second (often the last) as you close in.

Always imagine yourself as *coming* to the net or *taking* the net—never as rushing it.

Volleying

In your advance, pause before you volley. Do *not* volley on the dead run. Always get the first volley in, steadily. The game gets easier after that.

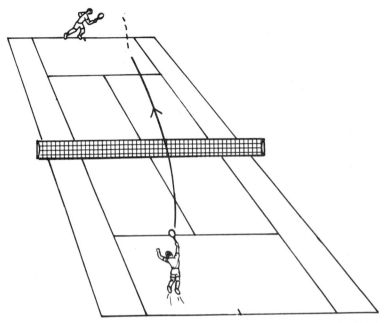

Illus. 36. FADING BACK TO SMASH A DEEP LOB TOWARDS YOUR BACKHAND SIDE: Your smash is safer if aimed as shown. Your racket face is more open (squarer to the ball). You have more court to hit into, over a low part of the net.

Smashing

The game gets easier after the first smash, more so than it does with volleying. To know this is a great incentive to play the first smash safely. Play it strongly enough, however, to force your opponent to lob again. His second (forced) lob is seldom as good as his first.

A deep lob over your backhand side is the most difficult one you can expect. If it is high enough to give you time to move to your left and make a forehand smash you should use this stroke, in preference to making only a defensive high backhand volley. In fading back in this way towards your backhand sideline, it is highly risky to attempt a sliced smash down your (right-handed) opponent's forehand sideline. You are aiming with a narrowed racket face and may mis-hit. Also, you are aiming at a narrow area and may miss it. Your slice will curve the ball, so that the alley rather than the court will be its natural target.

In contrast, see Illus. 36.

Comfortable Pattern

Play set after set consciously playing *your* game. Common sense will direct a variation here and there, but this will not disturb the comfortable pattern you settle into.

It sounds too easy, glib. All right, test it.

Coaches can coach you, friends can practice with you, experienced players can give you tips, well-meaning relatives can interfere, and, besides, you are your own analyst. It seems to be a full team, but all the time there's another member, if you notice him, giving you practical demonstrations. It's your opponent.

The next time you play, check him. If he's one who always beats you, without having better strokes than yours, you will recognize that his game is founded on the pattern we have discussed.

Anticipation

Watching the ball, you can still see your opponent. They are together in one mind's-eye picture at the other end of the court.

Your opponent can no more consistently disguise his intentions than you can. Over-concentrating on this, neither of you would be able to play properly. It follows, from your viewpoint, that there is plenty to be seen.

The first step in anticipation, however, is your own movement: as soon as you have hit your own shot, begin to move.

If you doubt the wisdom of this, on the grounds that often you may be in the best place anyway, try hitting a shot or two and remaining in place until the ball has landed. You will find yourself hurrying your next shot as a result, and that is the reverse of anticipation.

After hitting from near a sideline, move back towards center. After hitting one of your shots deep, be ready to move in a little, because your opponent's shot is likely to be shorter than usual. Position yourself in the center of possible returns. Take volleying as an example. (See Illus. 37 on the next page.)

If your opponent drops his racket head lower than for a drive, and all told can't help looking as though he is going to lob the ball, you should begin to ease back at once to cover it. If you wait until he has hit the ball it will sail over your head out of reach. Anticipation, not height, determines whether a player can cover lobs or is easy to lob over.

A player's cross-court and down-the-line forehands look different, and this difference can be seen before he hits the ball— that is, they are apparent in his setting himself and his backswing. Watch your next practice opponent and see for yourself. The difference is usually more pronounced with the backhand. As for those players who hit outside the ball for a cross-court backhand and use inside underspin to aim down the line, anticipating the direction of their shots is as easy as falling off a log. In all cases you are able to anticipate, to move before the ball is hit.

Many players throw the ball above their heads to serve their stock ball to your backhand. Trying for a surprise ace wide of your forehand in the right court, they throw the ball farther to their right. Anticipating this, you are more likely to score a down-the-line winner than to receive an ace.

Anticipatory signals are given all day long for you to see. Cultivate seeing them until you can't help seeing them.

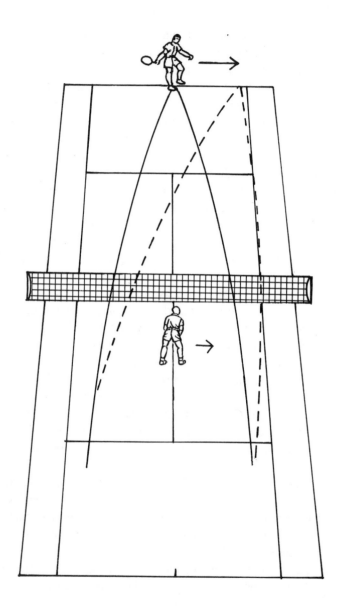

Try to blend everything into one smooth pattern: your strokes, your use of them, your preliminary anticipation in moving to the center of possible returns immediately after you have hit the ball, your final anticipation in moving before your opponent hits the ball.

(Opposite page)
Illus. 37. CENTER OF POSSIBLE RETURNS: Immediately after playing a shot to the center of opponent's court or to the side, an intending volleyer must position himself in the center of possible returns. Experience soon makes you a good judge of this position.

9. TACTICS

THE BASIS OF TACTICS is to bring your strength to bear on your opponent's weakness. If his backhand is the worst shot on the court: you play to it. If he is erratic and you are steady: you keep the ball in play and so give him maximum opportunity to err. If it's the other way round: you keep the ball away from him, to set up openings for yourself. If he is a volleyer: you keep the ball as deep as possible to restrict his chances of making approach shots. If you're the volleyer: you come in often on serve and return of serve and, whenever possible, you shorten his shots by taking them on the rise and sometimes on the full to make long volleys.

You know your own strength. Your opponent, unless you are outclassed, will reveal his weaknesses. If you see them only by the end of the match it may be too late, but do not despair. You will know them for next time because tennis players mostly recall their opponents' games. Also, you will come to spot weaknesses earlier with each opponent you play. You can notice a weak backhand or a wild forehand or an uncertain volley as early as during the warm-up period, so look for them.

The warm-up may show that your opponent is a confident strokemaker against high balls, and also that he hits forehands and backhands of normal height with strong topspin, meeting the ball noticeably far ahead of his front hip. He is a Western-style player. Your tactics, when the set starts, will be to play wide of him, keeping the bounce low if you can. His greatest weakness will be against balls you can get behind him.

You know you have weaknesses yourself, so be confident that your opponents have too. It is unrealistic for you to think otherwise of a player who approximates your own standard. Davis Cup players have weaknesses. They're pretty high-class ones, and it takes another Davis Cup player to exploit them, but that doesn't stop you from trying to spot them for your own education as you watch these players.

Obviously, the warm-up will show if your opponent is left-handed or two-handed. If he's left-handed, notice if he has a typical strong topspin forehand and dropped racket head backhand which he slides to your right-handed backhand. If so, you know to beware of his forehand and, taking the net against his backhand, that his two preferred shots will be a down-the-line pass and a lob. As for the man with the two-handed shot you can expect this to be solid but restricted in reach, so at once your tactics will be to try to spread him out. You can see how an understanding of tactics gives you confidence.

Suppose your opponent's strokes don't show you a single weakness. He hits smoothly from forehand and backhand at medium pace, he volleys nicely and his few practice serves look calm and controlled. Take heart, for unless he's out of your class, you're going to play well against him. His shots won't dip or kick or slither or slide and, what's more, he may be a complete stranger to the gentle art of scrambling to win a point. You are going to hit the center of your racket a lot more than usual. While you're about it, you're going to mix your game up as much as possible to try to hustle him about too. Tactics will not always win for you, but at least they make you think like a winner and that's a good start.

If you want to see tactics applied in high places you should watch the final of a big tournament. On occasion they are

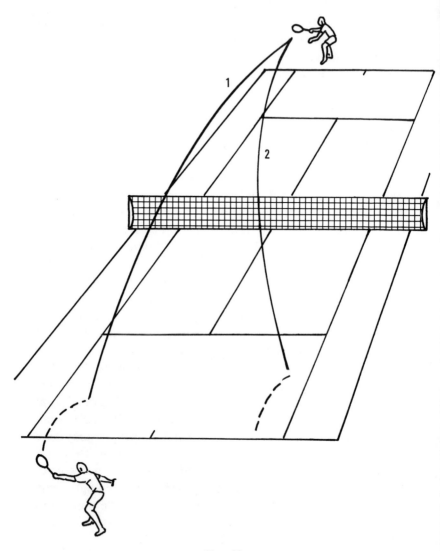

Illus. 38.

applied so rigidly that the match may become disappointing from the standpoint of stroke play. A player whose wonderful forehand you went to see may hardly have a chance to use it.

Returning to a more usual level, an interesting tactical battle usually results when two contrasting types of players meet. Player A is a right-hander with balanced forehand and backhand strength. Player B is a left-hander with a fierce topspin forehand and a strictly defensive backhand. They are playing a practice match under the eye of their coach. Here is the way he would order their tactics.

Left-hander, use that forehand every time you can. Run round every backhand you can. In a match don't hesitate about this. Right-hander, go for that backhand. Left-hander, keep farther over. Forget the center of possible returns for a moment, and protect that backhand of yours. Right-hander, play nearer to his backhand line. Left-hander, now he's getting slow and careful. You can get even closer to your backhand line and make forehands from his shots.

Right-hander, look out! He's enticing you to hit too close to the backhand line and fairly soon you'll be landing them in the alley and giving the points away. The best way to get at a man's backhand is to play first to his forehand, to force him to uncover a lot of backhand court and then play to his backhand and take the net. Take a swift look at Illus. 38.

But, left-hander, if he doesn't hit his first shot to your forehand deeply enough then the position suits you down to the ground. You have a ball on your forehand giving you a chance to take charge and then follow in to the net. You can play either of your two favorite forehands, which you know without looking are those shown in Illus. 39 on the next page.

Right-hander, you heard that. So play your shots deeply enough to stop him from taking charge. For most right-handers it is easier to make this first deep shot to your opponent's fore-

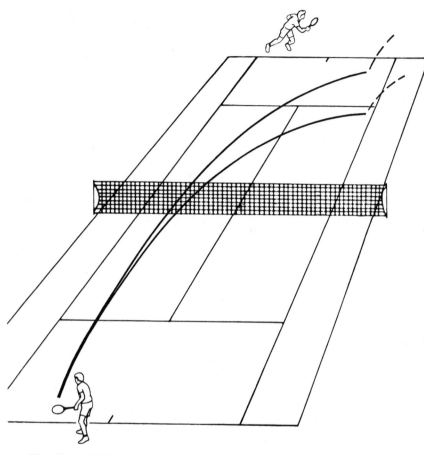

Illus. 39. A TYPICAL LEFT-HANDER'S TWO FAVORITE SHOTS: Often, when learning to play from the left doubles court, left-handers develop a wonderfully good topspin cross-court forehand drive. It plagues a right-hander, in singles or doubles.

hand against a left-hander than against a fellow right-hander. Your forehand goes down the line and your backhand goes cross-court on a long diagonal. You can get good depth naturally with both these shots.

Right-hander, now that you can pierce his backhand, follow in to the net. Left-hander, *don't* let him pin your backhand down. Attack harder with your forehand and *you* take the net . . .

Now imagine a real match between two such players meeting for the first time. If both know these tactics, they are in for a battle royal. If one does not, the other wins in a breeze. If it's the left-hander who doesn't know his business the poor fellow may decide he's not cut out for singles because his backhand is so vulnerable. If it's the right-hander, you'll probably hear him say in disgust that he never could play left-handers anyway.

Balanced Opponents

Here is a more usual case: a match between two right-handed players each being fairly well balanced in strength between forehand and backhand.

In the warm-up, the two appear evenly matched in stroke play, pace and ball control, yet throughout the ensuing match one player runs the other ragged. He has his opponent chasing from side to side while he himself seems to move only a few steps. Watching the game from above one end of the court, the winning player looks as though he is at the hinge of a pendulum, rocking his plumb-bob opponent from side to side. Both players hit the ball well. How does it happen?

It happens because one player is letting the other exploit long diagonals. (See Illus. 40 on the next page.)

In answer to Player A's first attacking drive, B should have returned the ball more or less along the direction of its line of

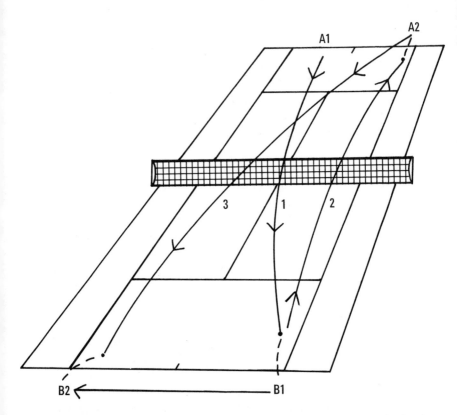

Illus. 40. DIAGONALS: Player A plays an attacking drive (1) to the forehand corner. Player B returns (2) down the line. Player A plays (3) a penetrating long diagonal and B begins his chase. If Player B plays his backhand down the line to A's forehand he is inviting another long diagonal forehand to his forehand corner. Here we leave him—in perpetual motion.

flight, but slower and well above the net, to give himself plenty of time to regain the center of his baseline. His thought in hitting down the line was that he was playing to his opponent's backhand. His mistake was in not knowing that in this position his opponent's backhand was better *placed* to deal a more effective blow than his somewhat stronger forehand could have.

Having made one mistake, it is by no means certain that B would learn a swift lesson and return A's diagonal in the correct way, that is, high, deep and about halfway between A's center mark and his backhand sideline. Chasing a wide and deep diagonal, it is easier to hit down the line than to make an extra effort to get farther behind the ball and play it back somewhat cross-court. Therefore, unless B knows something about tactics he can easily fall into the rôle of pendulum plumb-bob.

Remember these diagonals by thinking of them as deadly diagonals.

Use them, too, when you have the chance. You will have plenty of chances against those players who favor down-the-line shots from both forehand and backhand. Often you can recognize them in the warm-up. An almost certain clue is if their basic forehand and backhand are underspin drives. See Illus. 24 and Demonstration 4 again.

Against a more normal stroke-maker you can entice him into putting you in a position to play a deadly diagonal. (See Illus. 41 on the next page.)

Net Tactics

If you have a serve that your opponent can't handle, because of its power or twist or placement or anything else, come to the net behind it all the time. If your groundstrokes are no match for your opponent's, stake your game for the time being on a net attack—and then go away and work on those ground-strokes.

If you have a fair or good all-round game play all-court tennis. In effect, this means that you are always hunting for a net position that gives you a decidedly better-than-even chance of winning the point. This is sound tennis.

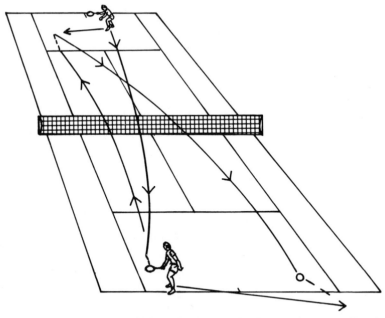

Illus. 41. CREATING A DIAGONAL: The ball is slightly towards your backhand side. You step round and make a forehand drive (1) to his backhand. (Don't hit it to his forehand corner, or he will have a forehand diagonal to your forehand corner.) Seeing your somewhat open forehand side he plays (2) down the line. At once you have a long diagonal (3) forehand to the forehand corner open to you.

For instance, you can come in on a good serve, but not on one you feel is not difficult for your opponent. Instead, you can rally, awaiting your chance of receiving a short ball and making a net approach from that. By the way, take your time with an approach shot and make a proper shot of it. Many players rush their approach shots, meeting the ball way out ahead of their bodies and getting no power and little direction out of an easy ball they have been given. This is a common fault. Take a shorter backswing than usual, but make a firm shot.

Court Surfaces

Much is made of champions' change of tactics to meet different court surfaces: that they play all-court tennis on clay and cement, hang back on a surface like rough asphalt, which slows down the ball's bounce, and go to the net on almost every ball on grass, shiny concrete and indoor wood or carpet. Lesser players should not be inflexibly governed by these tactics. As a general guide, a slower surface gives a driver a better chance to pass a net man, but if you give your opponent an awkward shot, such as getting the ball behind him, you should not be in the least inhibited. No matter how slow the court surface may be, you should take the net and reap the volley. Similarly, if you play on a very fast surface, it is still suicidal to take the net on a short ball.

Grass can be a fast surface if played on by fast players. Otherwise it is not as fast as is generally believed by people who do not play on it much. If you are not used to grass, the best advice concerns strokemaking rather than tactics. Do not stand up straight like a telegraph pole. Get well down to the ball by bending your knees sharply. This puts you in tune with grass-court play and prevents your being hopelessly weak on it.

Tactics for Points

All points are valuable, even the first one, the one farthest away from game. Nevertheless, you should play them differently, tactically. On game points and those one away from game point with a difference in the score of only one point or no difference (30–15, 15–30, 30–all, deuce) do not give your opponent a chance to make a winner with one shot. If he has a dangerous shot, keep away from it. Don't risk a drop shot you may miss or he may reach. If your second serve is weak, this is not the time to attempt an ace, but rather to place a medium first serve into play.

This gives a basis to follow, instead of not knowing what to do before the point starts.

Never Change a Winning Game

It would be sacrilegious to speak of tactics without including the master slogan, "Never change a winning game, always change a losing game." If you do not know this, you are highly likely to do the opposite in both cases: winning, there's always a temptation to do it another way as well; losing, you fear to change and lose worse.

Do not give up tactics that worry your opponent merely because you happen to make a mistake in finishing off the point. This sounds obvious, but it happens time and again with a player who lets himself become flurried. He sets everything up, takes the net, receives the easy volley he has worked for—and misses it. This happens again soon after. He then stays away from the net because he decides he's off his volley that day. If his reasoning is that he is changing a losing game, he certainly is confused. In fairness to the player though, this is rather an extreme case. It is more likely that he would give up going to the net after he has missed a couple of smashes, and doesn't want to risk having to attempt another one. It's the old story, that behind everything you need sound strokes.

10. MATCH PLAY FALLACY

IF MATCH PLAY is your weakness, it is very probable that you are certain it is nervousness, but it may be unsound strokes. Your symptoms are: you felt unreal, dazed, sick, too weak to hit anything; you were in front, but then collapsed; you played a set with a friend next day and hardly missed a ball. Your conclusion: no match temperament and you never will have.

Stop thinking you are Robinson Crusoe, the only one around. The same things and more have happened to thousands of people over tennis's hundred-year history. They only confirm that you are human and that all your systems function normally. Until you understand something of match play you can feel like this at any age and remain like it for the rest of your tennis life. As soon as you understand match play you will begin to change for the better.

■ Your strokes are not certain enough. They may be good with no pressure, but not good enough under the pressure of really wanting to win.

■ No one has yet seen a fighting type of match player without at least one stroke that was sound, even if no thing of beauty.

■ There is no good match player who cannot rely on any of his strokes and has no confidence in some of them.

■ Be critical of your strokes or any one of them, not of yourself.

■ As you gain true confidence in stroke after stroke your match temperament will respond accordingly.

■ You can work on your strokes directly, but can you do the same thing with your temperament? Your temperament will be influenced by your improved strokes. Your keenness to win will bring determination along with it.

Recommendations

■ Regard each match as another testing of your strokes. As they function, use them tactically.

■ When you lose, as distinct from your opponent genuinely beating you, blame some part of your game instead of yourself and work on it.

■ When you are genuinely beaten, learn your opponent's strengths. This is where you make great progress.

■ Try to enjoy playing matches, grimly if you like. Looking back, it's your match tennis you'll remember.

After many years of practical experience in play and observation, I say this advice applies to tennis. Bluntly, you're mad if you don't try it.

11. DOUBLES

DOUBLES IS A WEAKNESS of yours if you are underconfident before the game, or tentative in play, or your game deteriorates as the set or match approaches its final result.

Mostly, you can attribute any of this to your return of service.

It used to be said that the most important thing in doubles was a strong serve, and it was also thought that if you could volley well you would be a good doubles player. Without detracting from the merits of good serving and volleying it should be realized that both these strokes are backed by the advantage of position. In serving, you have the first hit and so can put your opponent at a disadvantage. You can also follow in to the net, making you and your partner the first pair there. Volleying, you have a position near the net and half the time the shot is set up for you by your partner.

In contrast, the return of service stands all alone and unassisted. It's the acid test.

Strong serving and dashing net interceptions are good play and build your confidence. However, for three-o'clock-in-the-morning courage, take the service return.

The team having the better service returns between them usually wins the match.

A player with a strong service return is never worried before a match about his coming performance. More often, he is anxious to get on the court to tear his opponents apart. At

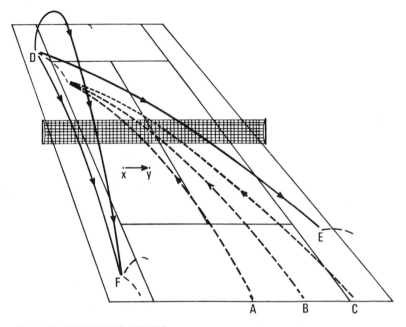

Illus. 42. RETURNS OF SERVICE
A-D-E: Server serves from near center mark A, to your forehand D. You return a short cross-court topspin shot to E, wide of his position.
B-D-F: Server serves from B, halfway between center mark and sideline, again to your forehand at D. Net man intends to intercept your return and moves from x to y. You play a passing shot down the sideline to F.
C-D-F: Server serves from C, wide, again to your forehand D. You lob over net man to F.

four-all and 30-all with the first service a fault, he is almost licking his lips. Contrast in your mind a tentative service-returner in the same situation at this score.

All of this means that if you are an underconfident doubles player the root cause is highly likely to be your return of service.

Attack with your service return whenever you can. This means you attack all second serves and as many firsts as possible.

Your attack can vary. If the server stays on the baseline your attack is usually a deep medium-paced shot followed to the net. If he does come in, the usual attack is a rising ball topspin drive, but instead you can play a low and slow shot to his feet. You can also attack the net man rather than the server by lobbing over his head or driving either down his sideline or down the middle.

When the first service is reasonably difficult, your service return has to be toned down to a controlled mark-time shot from which you hope to get a better opportunity to attack the next ball. When the first serve is really difficult (and fast but short is not difficult when within reach), your service-return has to be scrambled back. Know this and be prepared to do it. Do not slash at a very good serve. That is not attack, it is nothing. If anything it is quitting.

Your return of service is not one shot, it is many. (See Illus. 42.)

This illustration shows only the right court and only fore-hands and you will also realize that it is limited to the server's remaining on the baseline.

When the server takes the net and you attack him directly, your attack from forehand and backhand does not have to be similar. Many players attack, say, the second serve of an incoming server with a fast topspin forehand, but from their backhand with a low slice.

Rule out tentative service returns. You are only hoping for a blunder from your opponents. As the match progresses, and particularly near its end, you get worse and they get better. Hoping for mistakes is no basis for pre-match doubles confidence.

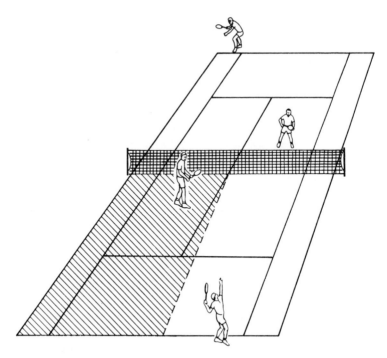

Illus. 43. NET MAN'S COURT COVERAGE: When the server follows his serve to the net, his net partner has to cover the whole of the shaded area—against center and sideline drives and against lobs.

Net Coverage

Assuming you have no worries with your strokes, you may still be underconfident before playing doubles and during play. You may vaguely think this is due to the presence of your partner, but, pinning it down, it is probably due to your uncertainty about net coverage when your partner is a server who always follows in to the net. (See Illus. 43.)

Have no further doubts. This is what you should cover, so with your good strokes go ahead and cover it. If your partner is a stronger player than you (or older, if you are young) do not be inhibited, but go ahead and cover this area yourself. If he is far weaker, stand farther back from the net and cover even more court. If he is only a little weaker, do not overdo things.

Conclusion

Make your stumbling blocks stepping stones, writes Father in Son's autograph book. Develop a mild complaint and nurse it, advised long-lived John D. Rockefeller. If you turn your weaknesses into strengths, you will receive the greatest satisfaction tennis can offer. Get your remedies right, then forge ahead.

INDEX